Vancouver
❄

Calgary
❄

Montreal
❄

Squaw
Valley
❄

Salt Lake
City
❄

St Louis
✳

Lake
Placid
❄

Los Angeles
✳

Atlanta
✳

Mexico
City
✳

Summer Olympic Games

Athens, Greece: 1896, 2004

Paris, France: 1900, 1924

St Louis, USA: 1904

London, England: 1908, 1948

Stockholm, Sweden: 1912

Antwerp, Belgium: 1920

Amsterdam, Holland: 1928

Los Angeles, USA: 1932, 1984

Berlin, Germany: 1936

Helsinki, Finland: 1952

Melbourne, Australia: 1956

Rome, Italy: 1960

Tokyo, Japan: 1964

Mexico City, Mexico: 1968

Munich, Germany: 1972

Montreal, Canada: 1976

Moscow, USSR: 1980

Seoul, Korea: 1988

Barcelona, Spain: 1992

Atlanta, USA: 1996

Sydney, Australia: 2000

Beijing, China: 2008

Winter Olympic Games

Chamonix, France: 1924

St Moritz, Switzerland: 1928, 1948

Lake Placid, USA: 1932, 1980

Garmisch-Partenkirchen, Germany: 1936

Oslo, Norway: 1952

Cortina d'Ampezzo, Italy: 1956

Squaw Valley, USA: 1960

Innsbruck, Austria: 1964, 1976

Grenoble, France: 1968

Sapporo, Japan: 1972

Sarajevo, Yugoslavia: 1984

Calgary, Canada: 1988

Albertville, France: 1992

Lillehammer, Norway: 1994

Nagano, Japan: 1998

Salt Lake City, USA: 2002

Turin, Italy: 2006

Vancouver, Canada: 2010

Beijing Olympic Games 2008

Melanie Guile

First published in 2008 by Heinemann Library,
an imprint of Pearson Australia Group Pty Ltd,
20 Thackray Road, Port Melbourne
Victoria 3207 Australia

Visit the Heinemann Library website
www.heinemannlibrary.com.au

© Pearson Education Australia 2008
(a division of Pearson Australia Group Pty Ltd,
ABN 40 004 245 943)

12 11 10 09 08
10 9 8 7 6 5 4 3 2 1

Commissioning: Michelle Freeman and Sarah Russell
Editorial: Eliza Collins
Cover and text design: Anne Donald
Map and diagram illustration: Anne Donald
Picture/permissions research: Wendy Duncan
Production: Tracey Jarrett

Typeset in Syntax 12/17 pt
Pre-press by Publishing Pre-press, Port Melbourne
Printed and bound by Craft Print International
Limited, Singapore
The paper used to print this book comes from
sustainable resources.

**National Library of Australia
Cataloguing-in-Publication data:**

Guile, Melanie, 1949- .
Olympic Games 2008: Beijing Olympic Games 2008.

Bibliography.
Includes index.
For primary school students.
ISBN 9781740703727 (hbk).

1. Olympic Games (29th : 2008 : Beijing, China) – Juvenile literature. 2. Beijing (China) – Juvenile literature. I. Title.

796.48

Acknowledgements

The publisher would like to thank the following for permission to reproduce copyright material: AAP Image/Anat Givon: p. **27**, /Dean Lewins: p. **23**; Corbis/Bettmann: p. **4**, /Grand Tour/Luca Da Ros: p. **8**, /Xinhua Press/Luo Xiaoguang: p. **16**; Getty Images: pp. **5**, **12**, /AFP: p. **13**, /AFP/Aris Messinis: p. **21** (upper), /AFP/Goh Chai Hin: p. **20**, /AFP/Roberto Schmidt: p. **7**, /Andrew Wong: p. **26**, /Andy Lyons: p. **18**, /Hassan Ammar: p. **25**, /Laureus/Kevin Lee: p. **6** (upper); Newspix/Craig Borrow: p. **21** (lower). All other images PhotoDisc.

Cover photograph of the Forbidden City, Beijing reproduced with permission of photolibrary/Alamy/ James Davis Photography.

Every attempt has been made to trace and acknowledge copyright. Where an attempt has been unsuccessful, the publisher would be pleased to hear from the copyright owner so any omission or error can be rectified.

Contents

Words that are printed in bold, **like this**, are explained in the Glossary on page 31.

Introduction

The Olympic Games are one of the world's most famous sporting competitions. Every four years, the best athletes from around the world compete for Olympic gold. The success of the Olympic Games is due to the efforts of one man – Baron Pierre de Coubertin.

Baron Pierre de Coubertin, 1863–1937, brought the Olympic Games to the modern world. His heart is buried at Olympia in Greece.

The 'father of the modern Olympics'

Baron de Coubertin lived in Paris, France, in the late 1800s. He read about the **ancient** sporting competitions that were held in Olympia, Greece, thousands of years ago. In these ancient contests, Greece's best athletes competed in running, jumping, throwing, wrestling, boxing and horse-racing events.

The baron wanted to introduce a modern form of the Olympic Games. He believed that they would bring countries together in peace and help to prevent wars. After years of planning, the first modern Olympic Games were held in Athens, Greece, in 1896. These games were the beginning of a great sporting tradition.

The modern Olympic Games

Since 1896, the Olympic Games have been held in a different country every four years. The members of the International Olympic Committee (IOC), which controls the Olympic Games, choose the host city. IOC rules state that only cities, not countries, can host the games. The next Olympic Games will be held in Beijing, China, in August 2008. Athletes from more than 200 countries are expected to compete.

Winter Olympic Games

The summer Olympic Games were so successful that the IOC decided to add new Olympic competitions. In 1924, the first winter Olympic Games were held in Chamonix, France, for snow and ice sports such as skiing and skating. At first, the summer and winter Olympic Games were held in the same year. But, since 1994, the winter games have been held in a separate year, halfway between the summer games. The next winter Olympic Games will be held in Vancouver, Canada, in 2010.

Paralympic Games

The Paralympic Games are for athletes with disabilities. The Greek word 'para' means 'beside' or 'alongside', so the Paralympic Games are played alongside the Olympic Games. The first truly Olympic-style games for people with disabilities were held in Rome, Italy, in 1960. The name 'Paralympic Games' was first used in 1984. Since 1988, each Olympic host city has held the Paralympic Games just after the summer Olympic Games, using the same **venues**. The Beijing Paralympic Games will be held in September 2008.

Olympiads

The four-year period between each Olympic Games is called an Olympiad. There have been 28 Olympic Games since 1896. The Games were not held in 1916, 1940 and 1944 because of World War I (1914–1918) and World War II (1939–1945). The Beijing Olympic Games in 2008 will be the Games of the 29th Olympiad.

China and the Olympic Games

In August 2008, the 29th summer Olympic Games will be held in the city of Beijing in China. These will be the first Olympic Games ever held in China, and every effort is being made to make sure they are a success. But, it is only since the 1980s that China has become one of the world's best Olympic nations.

China at the Olympic Games

In 1932, China sent its first Olympic athlete, **sprinter** Liu Changchun, to the Los Angeles Olympic Games in the USA. China continued to participate in the Games until 1949, when the **Communist Revolution** established the People's Republic of China. Taiwan, an island off mainland China, became anti-communist Nationalist China – so there were 'two Chinas'. For almost 20 years, Taiwan competed at the Olympic Games as 'China', but the much larger People's Republic of China did not compete. However, in 1984, with the encouragement of the USA and the International Olympic Committee (IOC), Communist China rejoined the games.

Chinese table tennis champion Deng Yaping has won four Olympic gold medals. Since her retirement from competition in 1997, Deng has worked on the Beijing Organising Committee for the Olympic Games (BOCOG), and is now the manager of the Olympic Village.

Olympic success

The 1984 Los Angeles Olympic Games in the USA were Communist China's first games in 20 years. They won 15 gold medals and came fourth in the overall number of medals won (medal tally).

Since then, China has continued to improve its performances, particularly in diving, shooting, swimming, gymnastics and table tennis. At the Athens Olympic Games in Greece in 2004, China won 32 gold medals, the second highest number, and came third in the overall tally. China hopes to top the medal tally in 2008.

Protests and human rights

Since Beijing won the Olympic **bid** to host the Olympic Games in 2001, the city has been transformed with spectacular sports venues and new roads, bridges and train lines. But, not everyone is happy. More than 100 000 homes have been demolished to make way for new Olympic **venues**. Other people complain about the huge cost of the Olympic Games, pointing out that two-thirds of Chinese people are poor. Protests have also been made against the Chinese Government's strict limits on free speech and religion. However, others claim that the Beijing Olympic Games will improve **human rights** as the country strives to gain international approval before the event.

The Beijing Paralympic Games

Beijing officials have said they want to increase opportunities for all disabled Chinese people through the Paralympic Games. During the 1990s, the Chinese Government improved the training facilities for disabled athletes. As a result, China is currently the world's best Paralympic nation, topping the overall medal tally in Athens, Greece, in 2004.

Star profile ★ Liu Xiang

Born 1983
Country China
Event Men's 110 metres hurdles
Achievements Became Olympic champion in the 110 metres men's hurdles in world-record time in Athens, Greece, in 2004. In 2006, Liu beat his own record when he clocked 12.88 seconds. He is a superstar in China and carries great hopes for gold at the Beijing Olympic Games.

Beijing the city

Beijing is in the north-east of China. It is a huge city of more than 15 million people. In August 2008, the eyes of the world will be on Beijing as it hosts the 29th Olympic Games.

Beijing the capital

Beijing is the capital of China. The government rules from Beijing, and the country's leaders live there. China's most famous educational and cultural organisations, such as Beijing University and the Beijing Opera and Ballet, are also based in the city. However, China has other great cities. Hong Kong, on the south-east coast, is one of the world's busiest ports. Wealthy Shanghai is the centre of China's largest banks and businesses. Guangzhou and Nanjing are known for their huge factories, mines and other industries.

History

The land around Beijing has been occupied for 500 000 years. A half-million-year-old human skeleton named 'Peking Man' was found there, as well as the remains of Stone Age tribes people. From around 1000 BCE, the town was an important military and trading centre. However, in 1403, Beijing became China's capital city when Emperor Chengzu moved his court there from Nanjing. Beijing became one of the world's greatest cities with magnificent temples and palaces. Today, Beijing is a crowded, modern city, and it is growing all the time.

Modern Beijing. The name 'Beijing' means 'northern capital'.

Geography

Beijing lies on the flat North China plain. Mountains rise to the north and west, and the sea lies 183 kilometres to the east. The city covers around 17 000 square kilometres. At its heart lies the famous public meeting place, Tiananmen Square, and the former Emperor's palace known as the Forbidden City. A series of ring roads encircle Beijing, and freeways connect the capital to other parts of China.

Climate

Winter comes to Beijing during the months of December to February, and summer is from June to August. Winters are cold and snowy, while summers are warm and wet. Late August and September, when the Beijing Olympic Games will be held, are usually sunny and mild.

Beijing average monthly temperature in degrees centigrade

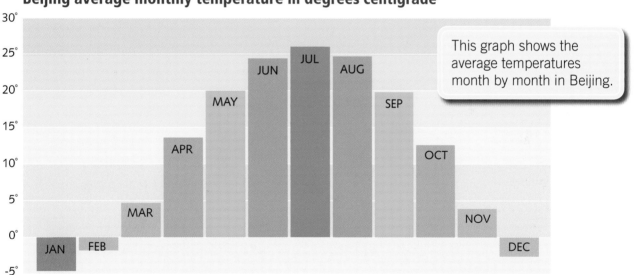

This graph shows the average temperatures month by month in Beijing.

Source: www.worldclimate.com

Pollution

Air **pollution** is bad in Beijing because lots of cars are driven in the city and there are many coal-powered **industries**. Dirty water is also a problem because industries and households pour waste into local rivers and lakes. The Chinese Government has promised to clean up Beijing for the Olympic Games in 2008.

Landmarks of Beijing

Beijing is home to five of China's 33 World Heritage listed sites, including the Forbidden City, the Great Wall, the Summer Palace, the Temple of Heaven and the Peking Man Ruins. There are approximately 200 other significant sites in the city too, including Tiananmen Square.

The Great Wall

The Great Wall of China runs north of Beijing. The first sections of the wall were built around 220 BCE to keep out invaders from Mongolia. Stretching 6400 kilometres west to east, the Great Wall is the world's largest man-made structure.

NORTH KOREA

SOUTH KOREA

Beijing

Yellow River

Wall

Great

NORTH

CHINA

PLAIN

Xi'an

(Ch'ang Chiang) River

Shi Highway

Peking Man Ruins

In 1929, a group of scientists working at Zhoukoudian near Beijing uncovered the 500 000-year-old skull of a Stone Age man. The discovery of 'Peking Man', as the remains were named, proved that humans developed over millions of years. The location of the find became famous, but fell into disrepair. However, the World Heritage site was repaired in 2007, just in time for the Beijing Olympic Games.

The Summer Palace
The Summer Palace was built in 1750 as a cool summer house for the emperor. It is surrounded by beautiful gardens, and sits on a hill overlooking Beijing. The Palace includes halls, temples, bridges and water features.

The Fifth Ring Road

The Fourth Ring Road

The Third Ring Road

The Second Ring Road

Airport Expressway

The Forbidden City
The Forbidden City is also known as the Imperial Palace and was begun in 1406. It was built as the home of China's ruling emperors. It is like a huge walled 'city', and includes magnificently decorated palaces, courtyards and artworks.

Tiananmen Square
Tiananmen Square is in the heart of Beijing. It covers 440 000 square metres and is the world's largest city square. Some of China's most important events have taken place here: Chairman Mao Zedong declared the People's Republic of China here after the Communist Revolution in 1949; and it was the site for the crushing of a huge rally for democracy in 1989, when many people were killed by government troops.

Temple of Heaven
The Temple of Heaven is a group of three marble and stone buildings first built in 1420. They were used by the emperor each year to pray for a good food harvest. The beautiful, round, three-storeyed Temple of Good Harvests is a famous Beijing landmark.

Jing-Jin-Tang Highway

Chinese culture at the Beijing Olympic Games

The official **mission** of the Beijing Olympic Games is to stage a 'high-level Olympic Games with **distinguishing features**'. This means Beijing is planning an outstanding games with a strong Chinese influence.

Distinguishing features

Logos and signs have the look of traditional Chinese ink and brush paintings. Official colours – such as 'Great Wall' grey – reflect Chinese landmarks. One of China's five Olympic **mascots** is Jingjing, the giant panda, which is China's most famous animal. His headdress is made of **lotus** leaves, a special plant in Chinese culture that stands for purity and perfection. The aim of these distinguishing features is to show China and its culture to the world.

The Olympic torch

The Olympic torch has the look of a curled-up Chinese paper scroll. It is decorated with red swirling clouds that stand for good luck. The torch is 72 centimetres long and made of aluminium.

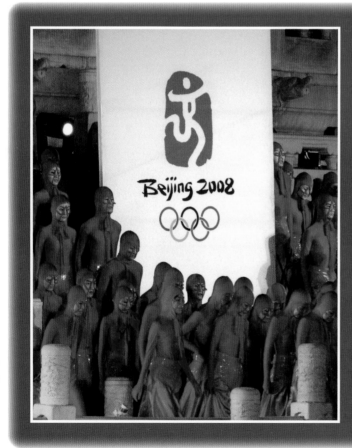

Olympic emblem

The Beijing Olympic **emblem**, or symbol, is titled 'Chinese Seal, Dancing Beijing'. It is based on the Chinese **seals**, or stamps, used on art and letters in **ancient** times. The shape of the dancing person is similar to the Chinese **character**, or sign, used in Chinese writing for 'Jing', which stands for 'Beijing'.

Mascots

There are five mascots – called *fuwa* in Chinese – for the Beijing Olympic Games, one for each ring on the Olympic flag. The Olympic rings themselves stand for the five regions that compete at the Olympic Games – Africa; the Americas; Oceania, including Australia; Asia; and Europe. The five *fuwa* names together say *Bei Jing Huan Ying Ni,* which means 'Welcome to Beijing' in Chinese.

Beibei the fish stands for **prosperity**, or wealth and success. She represents water sports and the blue Olympic ring.

Jingjing the giant panda stands for happiness. He represents strength and the black Olympic ring.

Huanhuan the Olympic flame stands for passion. He represents sporting spirit and the red Olympic ring.

Yingying the Tibetan **antelope**, or deer, stands for health. He represents speed and the yellow Olympic ring.

Nini the golden-winged swallow stands for good luck. She represents gymnastics and the green Olympic ring.

Lucky number

In Chinese culture, some days and years are especially lucky. The opening ceremony of the Beijing Olympic Games will begin at 8 o'clock on the night of 8 August 2008. In China, the number 8 is a symbol for success.

Olympic motto

The **motto** for the Beijing Olympic Games is 'One World, One Dream'. The motto means '**unity**, or togetherness; friendship; progress; **harmony**, or agreement; participation, or joining in; and dream'.

Beijing Olympic venues

This map shows some of the venues in and around Beijing where Olympic events will be held.

New venues

Thirty-two **venues** have been created in Beijing, 12 of them new. Most of these venues are to the north and west of the city centre. Transport has been improved, too, with 61 new roads, four new bridges and an extended underground railway system.

Not all Olympic events will be in Beijing. Sailing, football and horse-riding events will be held in six other cities, including Qingdao, Shanghai and Hong Kong.

Looking good

Like all Olympic cities, Beijing wants to show its best face to the world. In the lead-up to the Games, homeless people will be removed from the streets. Littering, spitting and **jaywalking**, or crossing the road illegally, will be banned. Beijing's people are even being taught how to queue quietly and smile at strangers!

The Tennis Centre is a new building. It is next to the archery and hockey fields, which are **temporary** venues that will be removed at the end of the Olympic Games.

The National Indoor Stadium will be used for gymnastics and handball.

The National **Aquatics** Centre is called the 'Water Cube' because its transparent blue walls look like an ice cube when lit from inside. The centre seats 11 000 people and will be used for swimming and diving events.

Jing-Shi Highway

The Laoshan **Velodrome** in west Beijing will host the cycling events. There is seating for 6000 people under its bowl-shaped roof.

Athletes will be housed in low-rise apartments in the Olympic Village. Officials have promised that it will take no more than 30 minutes to reach any venue in Beijing from the Olympic Village.

The Olympic Green is the main sporting area. It covers 1215 **hectares**. Fifty-six per cent of athletes will compete at the Olympic Green. Fourteen major venues are there, including the National Stadium, plus the Olympic Village and media centre. The Olympic Green also includes a 760 hectare forest park.

The Fifth Ring Road

The 91 000-seat National Stadium was designed by famous Swiss architects Jacqueline Herzog and Pierre De Meuron. It will be a spectacular setting for the opening and closing ceremonies and athletics events.

The Shunyi Olympic Rowing-Canoe Park is a newly built venue in north-east Beijing. It includes water courses made by humans, including **rapids**, for kayaking, canoeing and rowing events.

The Second Ring Road

The Third Ring Road

The Fourth Ring Road

The Olympic Sports Centre is a group of three venues at the southern end of the Olympic Green. These have been renovated for the games and include swimming and gymnastics facilities.

The Olympic Sports Centre Stadium has been remodelled for the games in a very modern style. It will be used for football (soccer) matches and some **pentathlon** events, such as running and horse riding.

Jing-Jin-Tang Highway

Facts and figures

China is spending a lot of money on the Beijing Olympic Games. However, Beijing officials are keeping the true cost of the Games a secret. Here are some other facts and figures about the Beijing Games.

Rebuilding Beijing

Massive new construction projects are being built in Beijing by a team of 67 000 workers. All **venues** are ahead of schedule, and will be finished in 2007, a year before the Olympic Games. New constructions include:

- 31 new or improved sports venues;
- 61 new roads;
- a new underground railway system; and
- a new airport **terminal** and runway.

The 'Bird's Nest'

The National Stadium is the main venue for the Beijing Games. It has been named the 'Bird's Nest' by locals because of its steel structure and shape. The stadium is 330 metres long and 220 metres wide, and its key features include:

- seating for up to 100 000 people (including **temporary** seats);
- 250 000 square metres of floor space; and
- 36 kilometres of steel **girders**, or rods, which were used in its construction.

Workers on the site of the National Stadium (the 'Bird's Nest'). The stadium includes 'green' features, such as rainwater collection and natural light.

Tourists

One million Chinese visitors and about 500 000 foreign tourists are expected in Beijing for the Olympic Games. About one million police and security guards will keep all **spectators** and residents safe.

Athletes and events

Athletes from more than 200 countries will compete in Beijing. In 2002, the International Olympic Committee (IOC) set limits on the size of the Olympic Games. The IOC allows 10 500 athletes to compete in 28 sports and 302 different events.

New events for the Beijing Olympic Games include a 10-kilometre **marathon** swim in open water and BMX (bicycle moto cross) races.

Volunteers

Each Olympic Games depends on its **volunteers** to make the event run smoothly. In Beijing, 70 000 volunteers will help out at the summer Olympic Games and 30 000 will be at the Paralympic Games. Two-thirds of these volunteers are from Beijing, and 80 per cent of them are under 30 years old. Most of the volunteers are university students. A lot is expected of them. Volunteers at the Beijing Olympic Games will research sporting facts and figures, interview athletes and write newspaper articles.

The torch relay

The Olympic torch will be lit at Olympia in Greece on 25 March 2008 and will pass through 28 cities in Greece, Italy, Egypt, Iraq, Iran and India before arriving in Beijing in time for the opening ceremony. These countries were chosen for their **ancient civilisations**. The torch will make history when it is carried to the top of the world's highest mountain, Mount Everest, before arriving in China. See http://torchrelay.beijing2008.cn/en/journey/map for details of the route of the torch relay.

A 'green' Olympic Games

Beijing has promised a 'green' Olympic Games, but this is a big task for one of the world's most **polluted** cities. To improve air quality, coal-burning factories have been closed or **converted** to cleaner energy. Four thousand **natural gas** buses have replaced polluting petrol-driven ones. Water and **sewerage** systems have also been improved. Today, 90 per cent of the city's toilet waste is treated, helping to clean up the city's rivers.

Summer Olympic sports

There are 28 official summer Olympic sports, but each sport may include different kinds of events. The sport of athletics, for example, includes running races, as well as jumping and throwing competitions. At the Beijing Olympic Games, 302 events will be held, including 165 men's events, 127 women's events and ten mixed (men and women) events.

New events for Beijing

Each host nation is allowed to choose one new sport to include in its Olympic Games. For instance, BMX bike events will feature for the first time in Beijing. Overall, nine new events will be held in 2008, including:

- 10-kilometre men's and women's open water swimming **marathons**;
- mixed team table tennis;
- 3000-metres women's **steeplechase**; and
- new women's fencing events.

The steeplechase

The steeplechase is a 3000 metres track race that includes 28 barriers, such as fences and water jumps. Kenyan Moses Kiptanui was the first to run the steeplechase in under eight minutes, achieving 7.58 minutes in 1995.

Athletics

Athletics are track-and-field sports such as running, walking, jumping and throwing. They have appeared at every modern Olympic Games since 1896. Athletics is also the largest Olympic sporting group, with 47 different events. In Beijing, athletics events will be held over the last ten days of the games at the National Stadium. The 100 metres **sprint** is always a highlight.

Star profile ★ Carolina Kluft

Born 1983
Country Sweden
Event heptathlon and pentathlon
Achievements World, Olympic and European heptathlon champion, Kluft is unbeaten in this event since 2002. Known for being a good sport, Kluft is popular with **spectators** wherever she competes. She is considered unbeatable in the heptathlon at the Beijing Olympic Games.

Athletics events

Athletics are divided into four groups – track, field, combined and road events. The field events include jumping and throwing contests. In combined events, each athlete competes in a number of different events. Road events are long-distance races held on open roads.

Group	Event	Distance	Men	Women
track	running	sprints – 100, 200 and 400 metres	✔	✔
		middle-distance races – 800 and 1500 metres	✔	✔
		long-distance races – 5000 and 10 000 metres	✔	✔
	hurdling	100 and 400 metres		✔
		110 and 400 metres	✔	
	relays	4 x 100 metres and 4 x 400 metres	✔	✔
	steeplechase	3000 metres	✔	✔
field	long jump		✔	✔
	high jump		✔	✔
	triple jump		✔	✔
	pole vault		✔	✔
	discus		✔	✔
	javelin		✔	✔
	shot-put		✔	✔
	hammer throw		✔	✔
combined	decathlon (ten events) – long jump, shot-put, discus, pole vault, javelin	100 metres sprint, 110 metres hurdles, 400 and 1500 metres running races	✔	
	heptathlon (seven events) – high jump, shot-put, long jump, javelin	100 metres hurdles, 200 and 800 metres running races		✔
road	race walk	20 kilometres	✔	✔
		50 kilometres	✔	
	marathon	42.195 kilometres running race	✔	✔

Summer Olympic sports

Archery

Archery is a sport that involves shooting at targets with bows and arrows. It has been an Olympic sport, off and on, since 1900. There will be four archery events at the Beijing Olympic Games.

Badminton

Badminton is an indoor sport played with round bats and a **shuttlecock**, or ball made of cork and goose feathers. In Beijing, there will be five events, which will be popular with **spectators** because China is a world-beater at badminton.

Baseball

Baseball is a team sport played with a club-like wooden bat and a hard ball. The game is the USA's national sport and very popular in the USA. Only one event – men's baseball – will be played in Beijing.

Basketball

Basketball is an indoor team game in which players score by throwing a large ball through a high hoop. Two events – men's and women's basketball – will be held in Beijing. Australia and China are very strong in women's basketball.

Star profile ★ Lin Dan

Born 1983
Country China
Event badminton
Achievements Ranked first in the world since 2004. Was unplaced at the Athens Olympic Games in Greece in 2004, but regained the world championship in 2006. Lin is a favourite to win gold at Beijing in front of his home crowd.

Boxing

Boxing matches were held at the **ancient** Olympic Games and have appeared at every modern Olympic Games since 1896. Matches are organised according to the weight of the boxers. Eleven boxing events – for men only – will be held in Beijing. However, women's boxing will be held at the London Olympic Games in England in 2012.

Canoe and kayak

Canoe and kayak races are held on both flat and rough water courses. Kayaks are closed-topped boats and canoes are open-topped. Sixteen canoe and kayak events will be held in Beijing – four for women and 12 for men. Women compete in kayak events only.

Cycling

Cycling events have appeared at every Olympic Games since 1896. There are four different kinds of cycling events – track, road, mountain bike and BMX – and 18 events altogether. Track events include the Madison, a 50-kilometre team race, and the Keirin, a 2-kilometre individual race. Road events are held for men and women. Mountain bike events involve races over hills and mountains, while BMX races are held on rough, hilly tracks.

Stuart McIntosh of Great Britain competing in the canoe singles during the 2004 Athens Olympic Games. Canoes and kayaks are paddled at a furious pace.

Star profile ★ Ryan Bayley

Born 1982
Country Australia
Event cycling
Achievements Won the **sprint** and Keirin cycling races at the Athens Olympic Games in Greece in 2004. Bayley is aiming for gold again in Beijing.

Summer Olympic sports

Equestrian

Equestrian, or horse-riding, events have been included in the Olympic Games since 1900. There are three types of events – jumping; dressage, which is a kind of horse-and-rider ballet to music; and three-day events consisting of dressage, jumping and a cross-country race.

Fencing

Fencing is a sport that grew out of sword fighting and has appeared at every modern Olympic Games. It features matches with three different kinds of blunt weapons – the lightweight foil, the heavier épée and the longer sabre. There will be ten fencing events in Beijing, including men's and women's individual and three-person team events.

World's greatest

The world's greatest fencer was Hungary's Aladar Gerevich (1910–1991), who won seven gold medals in six Olympic Games from 1932 to 1960. This is the longest winning streak of any Olympic athlete in any sport.

Football

Olympic football, also known as soccer, is one of the world's best-known games. It has been an Olympic sport since 1900. Two events – men's and women's football – will be held in Beijing.

Gymnastics

The sport of gymnastics highlights strength and artistic skill. There will be 18 men's and women's events in 2008, divided into trampoline, artistic gymnastics and rhythmic gymnastics. Artistic gymnastics covers 14 events and includes leaps on the **vault**, and dramatic swings and balances on the rings, beam, bars and **pommel horse**. Only women compete in rhythmic gymnastics, which features **acrobatic** movements to music using balls, ribbons, ropes, clubs and hoops. Trampoline includes one men's and one women's event.

Handball

Modern handball is a fast-paced indoor team game in which the ball is handpassed and thrown towards soccer-like goals. Men's and women's handball will be held at Beijing's National Indoor Stadium.

Hockeyroos aim to reclaim crown

The Australian women's hockey team, the Hockeyroos, won at the 1988, 1996 and 2000 Olympic Games. Disappointed to be placed fifth in 2004, the Hockeyroos are determined to win gold again in Beijing in 2008. However, competition will be tough against the current Olympic champions the Netherlands.

Hockey

Hockey is an outdoor team game played with curved sticks and a small ball. It requires skill and speed to score goals. Two events – men's and women's hockey – will be held in Beijing.

Judo

With 14 events, judo is one of the largest Olympic sports. It was invented by the Japanese who introduced it to the Olympic Games in Tokyo in 1964. Matches for men and women are graded for weight.

Modern pentathlon

The **modern pentathlon** was invented by Baron Pierre de Coubertin in 1912 and has appeared at the Olympic Games ever since. It consists of five contests – fencing, shooting, show jumping on horseback, a 200 metres swimming race, and a 3000 metres cross-country run. At the Beijing Olympic Games, there will be two events (men's and women's), each held over two days.

Rowing

Fourteen rowing events will be held at the Beijing Olympic Games. These include **sculls**, which are small racing boats with two oars for each rower, and larger boats with one oar for each person. Crews are made up of one, two, four and eight rowers.

Summer Olympic sports

Sailing

Sailing events for the 2008 Olympic Games will be held at Qingdao, a **port** about 800 kilometres from Beijing. Eleven men's and women's events will be held, in boats ranging from single-person sailboards to larger crewed boats.

Shooting

Shooting contests have been held at every modern Olympic Games. Olympic shooting includes five kinds of events – rifle, pistol and **air pistol**, plus skeet and trap. Fifteen shooting events for men and women will be held in Beijing.

Softball

Softball is an outdoor team game played with a club-like bat and ball that, oddly enough, is hard like a baseball. Just one event will be held in Beijing, and softball will be dropped from the Olympic Games after 2008.

Table tennis

Table tennis involves players batting a small, lightweight ball across a table. Four events (men's and women's singles and team events) will be held at Beijing in 2008.

Taekwondo

Taekwondo is a Korean sport sometimes called kick boxing. It is the world's fastest-growing self-defence sport. At the Beijing Olympic Games, eight taekwondo events will be held, organised by the competitors' weights.

Tennis

Tennis is one of the world's best-known games. It was played at the modern Olympic Games between 1896 and 1924, and then dropped because of the debate about the professional and/or amateur standing of the players. Tennis was reintroduced to the Olympic program in 1988. Four tennis events will be held in 2008 – singles and doubles for men and women.

Triathlon

Triathlon is a demanding swimming, cycling and running race that was introduced to the Olympic Games in Sydney in 2000. In Beijing, the triathlon will consist of a 1500 metres swim, a 40 kilometres cycle and a 10 000 metres run.

Born 1978
Country Iran
Event weightlifting
Achievements One of the world's strongest men, Hossein won the Olympic super heavyweight title twice (in Sydney in 2000 and in Athens, Greece, in 2004).

Volleyball

Volleyball, an indoor team ball game of handpasses and throws over a high net, has been an Olympic sport since 1964. However, since beach volleyball was introduced at the 1996 Olympic Games in Atlanta, USA, the sport has become an international sensation. The beach version is played outdoors on sand, and has two players to a side rather than six. There will be four volleyball events for men and women in Beijing.

Water sports

Aquatics, or water sports, have been held at every modern Olympic Games. There are four kinds of events – swimming races over a range of distances, diving, **synchronised** swimming and water polo. Swimming races are the largest group with 34 events. Eight diving events will be held at the Beijing Olympic Games. The Chinese are world diving champions, so tickets for this event will be popular.

Weightlifting

Men's weightlifting events were held in the 1896 Olympic Games, but women's events were introduced only in 2000. The Beijing Olympic Games will have 15 men's and women's events, which are organised according to the weight of the lifter.

Wrestling

Men's wrestling has appeared at every modern Olympic Games. However, women's wrestling was new to the Olympic Games in 2004. Eighteen events will be held in Beijing, 14 of them for men.

The Beijing Paralympic Games

The 13th Paralympic Games will be held in Beijing from 6 to 17 September 2008, exactly 13 days after the summer Olympic Games end. Paralympic events are hard-fought and exciting, and are becoming increasingly popular with **spectators**.

Classification

There are six groups of disabilities in the Paralympic Games:

- amputee (missing an arm or leg);
- cerebral palsy (physical disability caused by damage to the brain);
- visual impairment (blind or partly blind);
- **spinal cord** injuries (limited use of legs and/or arms);
- intellectual disability (mentally impaired) – this category has been banned from the Paralympic Games since 2000 because of cheating; and
- *les autres*, which is a French term that means 'the others' or, in this case, other kinds of physical disability, such as people with the disease multiple sclerosis.

The athletes

Four thousand Paralympic athletes from around 150 countries will compete in Beijing for 471 gold medals. Following International Olympic Committee rules, Paralympic events will be held in the summer Olympic Games **venues**, and athletes will stay in the Olympic Village.

Fu Niu Lele the cow is the Paralympic **mascot**. She stands for determination, hard work and a positive attitude, which are just some of the qualities shown by Paralympic athletes.

26

China's Paralympic record

China is one of the world's best Paralympic nations. At the Athens Paralympic Games in Greece in 2004, China topped the tally with 141 medals, 63 of them gold. Its proudest moment came when Chinese athletes won gold, silver and bronze in one of the women's track cycling events. It is expected that China will field the largest Paralympic team in Beijing, and top the medal tally again.

Sang Lan is a popular spokesperson for China's Paralympians. A former champion gymnast, Sang broke her spine at a competition in 1998 when she was 17 years old and now uses a wheelchair. Sang is a **Goodwill Ambassador** for the Beijing Paralympic Games.

Paralympic sports

There are 20 sports on the Paralympic Games program. Rowing is a new Paralympic event in 2008.

archery

athletics

boccia (an indoor sport, rather like lawn bowls, developed for physically disabled people)

cycling

equestrian

football (two sports: five a side and seven a side soccer teams)

goalball (a three-person team sport played on an indoor court in which blind or blindfolded players roll the ball to the other team's side to score goals)

judo

power lifting (a form of weightlifting)

rowing

sailing

shooting

swimming

table tennis

volleyball

wheelchair basketball

wheelchair fencing

wheelchair rugby

wheelchair tennis

Countdown to Beijing timeline

This timeline shows the history of China's involvement with the Olympic Games and the key events leading up to the Beijing Olympic Games in 2008.

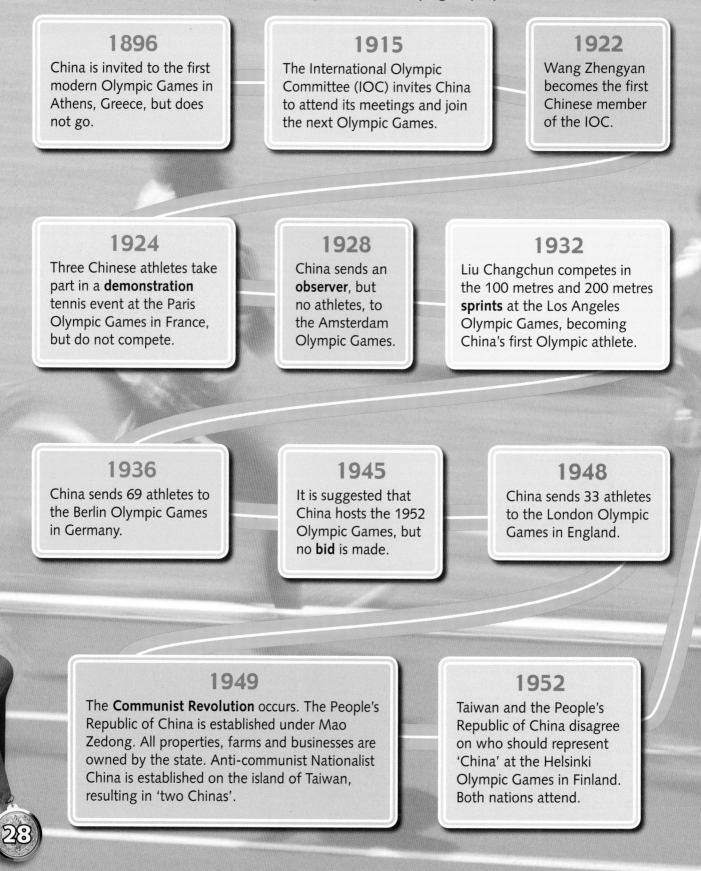

1896
China is invited to the first modern Olympic Games in Athens, Greece, but does not go.

1915
The International Olympic Committee (IOC) invites China to attend its meetings and join the next Olympic Games.

1922
Wang Zhengyan becomes the first Chinese member of the IOC.

1924
Three Chinese athletes take part in a **demonstration** tennis event at the Paris Olympic Games in France, but do not compete.

1928
China sends an **observer**, but no athletes, to the Amsterdam Olympic Games.

1932
Liu Changchun competes in the 100 metres and 200 metres **sprints** at the Los Angeles Olympic Games, becoming China's first Olympic athlete.

1936
China sends 69 athletes to the Berlin Olympic Games in Germany.

1945
It is suggested that China hosts the 1952 Olympic Games, but no **bid** is made.

1948
China sends 33 athletes to the London Olympic Games in England.

1949
The **Communist Revolution** occurs. The People's Republic of China is established under Mao Zedong. All properties, farms and businesses are owned by the state. Anti-communist Nationalist China is established on the island of Taiwan, resulting in 'two Chinas'.

1952
Taiwan and the People's Republic of China disagree on who should represent 'China' at the Helsinki Olympic Games in Finland. Both nations attend.

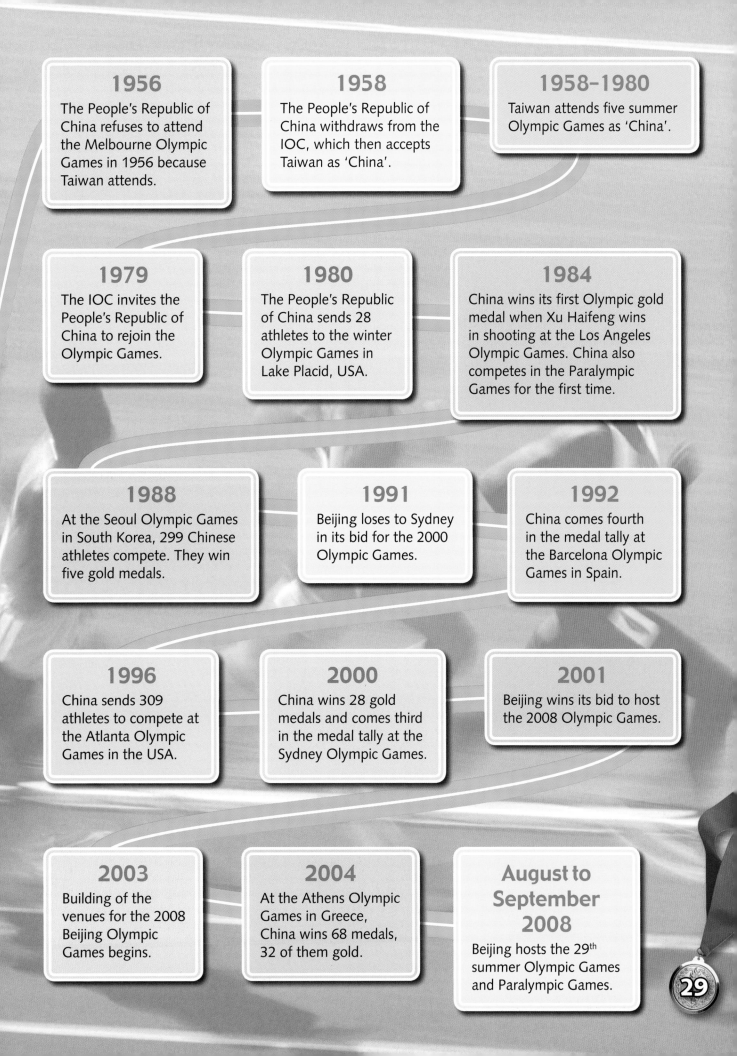

1956

The People's Republic of China refuses to attend the Melbourne Olympic Games in 1956 because Taiwan attends.

1958

The People's Republic of China withdraws from the IOC, which then accepts Taiwan as 'China'.

1958–1980

Taiwan attends five summer Olympic Games as 'China'.

1979

The IOC invites the People's Republic of China to rejoin the Olympic Games.

1980

The People's Republic of China sends 28 athletes to the winter Olympic Games in Lake Placid, USA.

1984

China wins its first Olympic gold medal when Xu Haifeng wins in shooting at the Los Angeles Olympic Games. China also competes in the Paralympic Games for the first time.

1988

At the Seoul Olympic Games in South Korea, 299 Chinese athletes compete. They win five gold medals.

1991

Beijing loses to Sydney in its bid for the 2000 Olympic Games.

1992

China comes fourth in the medal tally at the Barcelona Olympic Games in Spain.

1996

China sends 309 athletes to compete at the Atlanta Olympic Games in the USA.

2000

China wins 28 gold medals and comes third in the medal tally at the Sydney Olympic Games.

2001

Beijing wins its bid to host the 2008 Olympic Games.

2003

Building of the venues for the 2008 Beijing Olympic Games begins.

2004

At the Athens Olympic Games in Greece, China wins 68 medals, 32 of them gold.

August to September 2008

Beijing hosts the 29th summer Olympic Games and Paralympic Games.

Find out more

Using the Internet

Explore the Internet to learn more about the venues, events and people featured in this book. Websites can change so if the links below no longer work, use a reliable search engine, such as http://yahooligans.yahoo.com or http://www.kids.net.au, and type in the keywords, such as the name of a person, place or event.

Websites

http://en.beijing2008.cn
The official website of the Beijing Olympic Games covers every aspect of the Beijing games, including athlete profiles, sports, venues, mascots, environmental issues, latest news and dozens of links. It features an education page with stories and information that will be of interest
to students.

www.beijingpage.com
The Beijing Page is a useful site with hundreds of links. Topics include general information about Beijing and its attractions, photo galleries, and even blogs and forums about life in the city.

www.paralympic.org
The official website of the International Paralympic Committee (IPC) features a wide range of information on the Paralympic Games, including history, details of all Olympic results, issues and news reports.

Books

Middleton, H. *Modern Olympics* Heinemann Library, Oxford, 2004
This book explores the modern Olympic Games and features in-depth profiles of particular jobs and roles at the Games.

Pellegrini, N. *Beijing* (*Global Cities* series) Evans Publishing, London, 2000
This book provides information about one of the world's global cities, from why it is located where it is to the challenges presented by its enormous and growing population.

Renner, C. *Follow the Dream* series Echidna Books, Port Melbourne, 2004
This series provides information about how Australia's athletes achieve Olympic selection and what life is like for them in the lead up to and during the Olympic Games.

Glossary

acrobatic involving leaps, somersaults and other movements

air pistol type of gun powered by air pressure

ambassador important person who represents a state or organisation

ancient very old; in a time long past

antelope kind of deer

aquatics water sports

BCE stands for 'before the common (or current) era' and replaces the old term, BC ('before Christ'). Year 1 is the traditional birth of Jesus Christ. BCE years are the years before year 1, and are counted backwards; for example, 1300 BCE is 1300 years before the birth of Christ.

bid offer or claim for something

character single word or sign in the Chinese written language

civilisation advanced and complex culture

communist person who believes in a political system in which most property is publicly owned and each person works for the benefit of all in the community or state

converted changed over

demonstration sporting event held for general interest, not in competition

discus heavy, round, flat disc

distinguishing features outstanding, unusual or unique elements

emblem a sign or symbol

equestrian horse-riding events

girders heavy, strong bars used in building

goodwill good or positive feelings

harmony agreement

hectare an area of land of 10 000 square metres

human rights rights and freedoms that all human beings should have; for example, the right to freedom of speech and religion

industry a particular business

javelin lightweight spear

jaywalking crossing a street in an illegal way

Latin ancient language of Rome

logo graphic sign, symbol or brand

lotus water plant regarded highly in Chinese culture

marathon extra-long race

mascot object or animal thought to bring luck

mission official statement of goals or aims

motto words expressing an ideal

natural gas fuel found naturally underground that is less polluting than some other fuels

observer person who watches but does not participate

pentathlon (modern) five-event sport in which athletes must compete in shooting, fencing, swimming, horse riding and running events

pole vault high-jump event in which extra height is gained by using a long, flexible pole

pollution wastes that make things, like the air, waterways and the land, dirty

pommel horse equipment used by male artistic gymnasts involving swings of the legs

port a sea port, a destination for ships

prosperity wealth and success

rapids part of a river where the water is fast flowing

revolution complete and dramatic change to a new form of government

sculls small racing boats with two oars for each rower

seal stamp used long ago to seal or mark important documents

sewerage toilet waste

shot-put heavy metal ball used for throwing

shuttlecock feathered ball used in badminton

spectators people watching an event

spinal cord nerve centre of the human body running inside the spine

sprint short, fast race

steeplechase running race in which obstacles, such as fences and water jumps, are placed around the track

synchronised done at exactly the same time

temporary lasting for a time only

terminal (airport) an airport, a destination for aircraft

unity togetherness

vault equipment used by gymnasts to make leaps and somersaults

velodrome round indoor track used in cycling races

venue place specially designed for playing sport

volunteer a person who does work for no pay

31

Index

Lillehammer
Oslo
Stockholm
Helsinki
Moscow
Amsterdam
London
Berlin
Antwerp
St Moritz
Paris
Munich
Chamonix
Garmisch-Partenkirchen
Albertville
Innsbruck
Grenoble
Sarajevo
Turin
Cortina-d'Ampezzo
Barcelona
Rome
Athens
Olympia
Beijing
Sapporo
Seoul
Nagano
Tokyo
Sydney
Melbourne

N

Summer Olympic Games
Winter Olympic Games

0   2000   4000 km